Many cultures in the world learn best through imagery portrayed in songs, poems, art, parables, and stories. In Images of Leadership, Dave Bremner fills a gap in Christian leadership teaching, which is otherwise highly abstract. This book not only brings to prominence significant biblical ideas of a leader and how they should lead, it also unveils a visual language that will awaken our understanding of those biblical images. Such visual language is 'spoken' by every culture and is highly relevant for leading today's multi-cultural teams. I highly recommend this book to all those who want to lead and be led well.

Dr Joshua Bogunjoko
International Director, SIM

A treasure lies within this book. Having heard Dr. Bremner, I can attest to its distinctive value. Combining picture and text energizes personal reflection and growth. Beyond that is the invigorating discussion this book can stimulate in a group study. Imagine life-giving insights as the Holy Spirit speaks from each to all, through engaging image, text and life experiences.

Dr Duane H. Elmer
G. W. Aldeen Chair of International Studies, retired
Distinguished Professor of Educational Studies, Emeritus
Trinity International University/Evangelical Divinity School

In a world filled with power seeking leadership—even within the church—and, in which the ancient serpent of Genesis and Revelation continues to deceive humanity by questioning and distorting God's words, Dave Bremner's work is a refreshing reminder that Jesus has modeled for us the character and essence of godly leadership. This is a beautiful book of word and pictures, pointing us to Jesus and to the only pathway to lead effectively— Shepherd, Servant, and Steward—for God's mission in the vast diversity of human life and culture.

Dr Sherwood Lingenfelter
Senior Professor and Provost Emeritus,
Fuller Theological Seminary

What does leadership look like in God's Kingdom? This book explores the familiar images of a shepherd, servant and steward through a biblical lens. It speaks honestly about the dangers and messiness of leadership, yet points to the ultimate purpose of leadership: to grow into what God has designed us to be — like Christ.

Rev Dr Patrick Fung
General Director, OMF International

Amidst a plethora of writings on leadership, Dave Bremner invites the reader to ponder the timeless images of shepherd, servant and steward exemplified in the sacrificial life of Jesus. Shared leadership in God's Kingdom is creatively portrayed through photography and practical wisdom that counters the pursuit of power and privilege often promoted by the kingdoms of this world. *Images of Leadership* is timely for those who wish to deepen their leadership effectiveness through following Jesus.

Dr Roger Heuser
Professor of Leadership Studies, Vanguard University

Images of Leadership echoes the model of Jesus who led by example. It beautifully and deeply addresses the real life of a Christian leader that Jesus mandated his followers to be – shepherds, servants, stewards and leaders who share leadership. You will find no other book that has skillfully delved into Scripture and unearthed gems of wisdom. It will transform your life, your leadership skills and the lives of those you lead.

Dr Robert M. Kamau
President and Founder of African Transformational Leadership

The lack of godly leadership results in a disastrous scenario where the flock is scattered and, without proper care, could slip into the darkness. The book offers a wealth of biblical and practical insight into the images of a shepherd, servant and steward for leaders who long to be faithful in their call to lead God's flock placed under their care. Dave Bremner has brought us back to the biblical roots of leadership as found in both the Old and New Testament.

Rev Dr Siegfried Ngubane
Regional Director for Southern Africa, SIM

With conciseness, clarity and a deep commitment to Scripture, Dave Bremner has produced a must-read leadership guidebook. Using the biblical prescriptions of shepherding (loving the people under our care), servanthood (humble love lived out), and stewardship (faithfully pursuing God's agenda), Dave challenges our motives and stimulates our faithfulness. Whether we are pastors, ministry leaders or parents investing in the next generation, *Images of Leadership* will catalyze greater Christ-like leadership.

Paul Borthwick
Senior Consultant, Development Associates International

The world needs leaders who exemplify the values of God's Kingdom. Through the biblical imagery of the shepherd, servant and steward, the author prudently inspires such needed leadership. This timely publication underscores how leaders are intrinsically interconnected with those they lead.

Dr Stephen Coertze
Executive Director, Wycliffe Global Alliance

There is a global crisis of confidence in leadership, with trust in leaders in short supply. This book draws us into God's desire for leaders to follow after his heart. Don't be fooled by the beautiful images in this book. There are no shortcuts; it's counter-cultural. But these images of leadership will enable people and God's leaders to flourish.

Dr Paul Bendor-Samuel MBE
Executive Director, Oxford Centre for Mission Studies

Not many have thought as deeply, as biblically, as globally and as practically about leadership as Dave Bremner. As one who has benefitted greatly from Dave's faithful and faith-filled leadership as well as from his years spent reflecting on how to develop the leadership of others, I am delighted that his meditation on this vital topic is now available to a wider audience — and in such a creative and visually compelling way.

Dr Steven M. Bryan
Professor of New Testament, Trinity Evangelical Divinity School

Images of Leadership is brilliantly and creatively written. A must-read for anyone who is serious about leading God's way.

Dr Lawrence Tong
International Director, OM International

IMAGES OF
LEADERSHIP

BIBLICAL PORTRAITS OF GODLY LEADERS

Dave Bremner

Images of Leadership: Biblical Portraits of Godly Leaders

Paperback:
ISBN-13: 978-1-59452-781-4
ISBN: 1-59452-781-4

Hardcover:
ISBN-13: 978-1-59452-782-1
ISBN: 1-59452-782-2

Published by Oasis International Ltd, in partnership with SIM.
To find out more about SIM visit www.sim.org

Oasis International is a ministry devoted to growing discipleship through publishing African voices.
- We *engage* Africa's most influential, most relevant, and best communicators for the sake of the Gospel.
- We *cultivate* local and global partnerships in order to publish and distribute high-quality books and Bibles.
- We *create* contextual content that meets the specific needs of Africa, has the power to transform individuals and societies, and gives the Church in Africa a global voice.

Oasis is: *Satisfying Africa's Thirst for God's Word*. For more information go to oasisinternational.com.

21 22 23 24 25 26 27 28

TABLE of CONTENTS

FOREWORD

The effectiveness of any organization depends on the quality of its leadership. The survival of an organization depends on the quality of its leadership development. Yet so many organizations, even Christian organizations, are permeated with ineffective leaders. A classic study on missionary attrition attributed leadership tensions as the primary cause for leaving. The primary difficulty doesn't seem to be lack of leadership skills, management techniques, or even crosscultural sensitivity, but an unhealthy understanding of leadership.

David Bremner is the ideal person to write this book. I first met Dave when he served as a church-planting veterinary doctor in Paraguay. He ministered together with his wife Nikki in one of the most resistant unreached areas in Latin America. As the visiting International Director of SIM, I observed Dave for several days and was deeply impressed by how this young missionary was being used of the Lord to gain the trust of the local people as he took care of their cattle and graciously shared the Gospel. I saw how he interacted with people, his vision for the ministry and his cultural sensitivity. Before I left, I told him that

I detected solid leadership qualities in him. Soon he was selected to be the field director for Paraguay and then International Deputy Director. Others also saw in Dave a shepherd, servant and faithful steward.

More recently Dave has been leading one of the best leadership development programs I've experienced. He, Nikki and his team have developed a multicultural leadership mentoring program that is outstanding. I've participated with Dave in four cycles as a mentor to leaders from four very different cultures. I've watched as Dave taught concepts from *Images of Leadership* to newer, growing leaders, and have been awed by how these leadership principles have begun to permeate the ethos of the mission.

James E. Plueddemann, Ph.D.
Former International Director of SIM, and missionary with SIM in Nigeria.
Retired Professor of Missions and Intercultural Studies at Trinity Evangelical Divinity School (IL) and former Professor of Intercultural Education at Wheaton College (IL).
Author of Leading Across Cultures *and* Teaching Across Cultures *(IVP).*

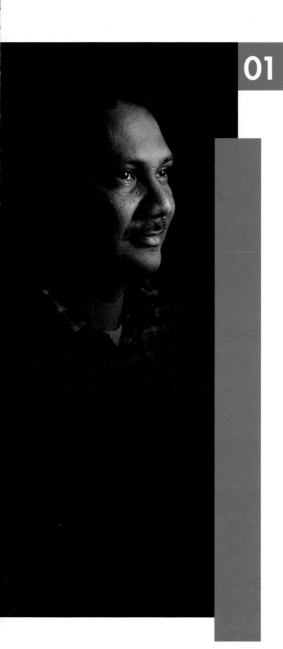

IMAGES OF LEADERSHIP

What should leadership look like in God's Kingdom? How does a leader behave and lead in a way that pleases God?

An intriguing cluster of rich images in the Bible conveys God's answer to these questions. These pictures are remarkably complex, and yet the profile they unveil is easy to grasp. They reveal, with an amazingly simple clarity, how we can lead in a way that pleases God.

Understanding leadership can be frustrating and elusive. The constant flood of books and articles on leadership testifies to the fact that the practice of leadership remains a challenge for each generation. The difficulties are highlighted in our lives every day as we observe examples of leadership around us. In our own homes, our places of work, multinational businesses, and on the world stage of celebrities and politicians, we see both good and bad, helpful and disastrous, positive and destructive results from the ways people lead. Publications borne of solid research in the marketplace have provided a wealth of ideas on how to lead well. Although these can be very informative for those who are followers of Christ, some of the approaches may reflect values that are not entirely helpful to believers.

In the gospels, Jesus uses the term "the Kingdom of God" many times to indicate the extent of God's reign in the world. All those who form part of the redeemed world and who willingly submit to God's authority

Luke 13

18 *He said therefore, "What is the kingdom of God like? And to what shall I compare it?*
19 *It is like a grain of mustard seed that a man took and sowed in his garden, and it grew and became a tree, and the birds of the air made nests in its branches."*
20 *And again he said, "To what shall I compare the kingdom of God?*
21 *It is like leaven that a woman took and hid in three measures of flour, until it was all leavened."*

Isaiah 64

8 *But now, O Lord, you are our Father; we are the clay, and you are our potter; we are all the work of your hand.*

Isaiah 66

13 *As one whom his mother comforts, so I will comfort you; you shall be comforted in Jerusalem.*

Psalm 144

1 *Blessed be the Lord, my rock, who trains my hands for war, and my fingers for battle;*
2 *he is my steadfast love and my fortress, my stronghold and my deliverer, my shield and he in whom I take refuge, who subdues peoples under me.*

and reign are included in his kingdom. His kingdom is both already present and not yet complete. A day is coming when his kingdom will be fully revealed and whole. Until then, it encompasses all who earnestly desire to be led by him and submit to his personal reign over their lives. Leadership in his kingdom thus includes all who lead within his rule on earth, whether in specific congregations of believers or in enterprises dedicated to his purposes on earth. This kingdom, which already exists but is still to come, is made up of broken but redeemed people who are all wrestling with their humanity. As such, it is most definitely a long way from perfect or even attractive, but it is made up of people who are being made new into the likeness of Christ. Leadership in this kingdom remains messy, fraught with dangers and failures, and yet hopeful in the power of the Holy Spirit who resides in each member.

The question we ask then is: How do I as a believer and a follower of Jesus lead his church, or his ministry, so that he is pleased with my leadership? We can also ask: How do I as a follower of Jesus lead those who don't yet know him in a way that truly reflects his character? Jesus often uses stories to communicate the profound truths of his kingdom. Many of his parables start with the simple question: "What can we compare the Kingdom of God to?" He then unwraps a story that lucidly reveals a hidden truth of the very real world of the spirit. A narrative, a metaphor, or a comparison can sketch the unseen reality of the spirit in pictures we can understand.

Effective communication starts with what is familiar and then builds new knowledge on to what is already understood. In order to communicate the eternal truths of God and his purposes, the Scriptures use familiar things in our earthly lives to help us understand the unseen realities of God and his purposes.

An enormous chasm must be bridged between what we as human beings can comprehend and the reality of who God is. The infinite span between God and humanity is expressed this way by Isaiah: "For as the heavens are higher than the earth, so are my ways higher than your ways and my thoughts than your thoughts" (Isaiah 55:9). Throughout both the Old and the New Testaments, the Bible communicates across this chasm using similes and metaphors rooted in human experiences. They provide windows through which we can glimpse God's ways and thoughts. God's relationship with us is portrayed in concepts so familiar that we immediately form vivid pictures in our minds of what he is like. He is our loving father, our comforting mother, our king, our shield, and our fortress. He is a consuming fire, a loving bridegroom, a powerful master, and a close friend. His power is like the untamed magnificence of storms, lightning, and earthquakes. His voice resounds like

> *God's relationship with us is portrayed in concepts so familiar that we immediately form vivid pictures in our minds of what he is like.*

thunder, whispers like a gentle breeze, and commands into being that which did not exist before.

The carefully woven thread of the images of leadership in the Bible conveys God's views on how we should lead and how we should follow. These images are not suggestions to enhance our capacity as leaders. They are not optional approaches, and they do not represent an opinion on the topic of leadership. They are instructions on how God expects us to lead under his reign. The mighty people memorialized in human history for their accomplishments don't

always measure up to the images we find in Scripture. Powerful statesmen have led nations to great accomplishments, often through the force of their personalities, their character, and their unbridled ambition. Others have toppled empires and governments through the gentle yet unyielding nature of their passive resolve. Business tycoons have achieved immense wealth and acclaim through their unfettered determination and brilliance. We tend to equate these celebrated people with good leadership, so it is easy to assume their techniques and successes will lead to effective leadership in God's Kingdom on earth.

However, we would be deceived if we allowed those examples to guide our approach to living and leading like Jesus. The biblical images of God-pleasing leadership paint quite a different picture.

The Bible's pictures of leadership are not mere illustrations of good leaders; they are prescriptions for how leadership is to operate in God's kingdom.

How then should we lead?
What does leadership look like in the Kingdom of God?

Well, it looks very much like a shepherd caring for his flock of sheep.

It looks like a dedicated servant of the master, serving those entrusted to him.

It looks like a steward of someone else's wealth and resources, but who dedicates his very life to caring for them on behalf of the true owner.

Each picture illustrates the characteristics of the same leader, not three different leadership styles. Jesus lives out these images as he invests in his disciples, teaches them, and equips them to lead the greatest enterprise in all of history. He embraces the roles prepared for him since God spoke the universe into being. Jesus is the good shepherd, the humble servant, and the faithful steward.

We are called to lead in the same way. The Bible's pictures of leadership are not mere illustrations of good leaders; they are prescriptions for how leadership is to operate in God's Kingdom. Each image has its own particular embedded value that defines godly leadership. These values speak into the lives of leaders at home, at work, in ministry, and in their local church.

The three images find full expression in Paul's teaching on the body of Christ, in which each member of the body uses his gifts for the benefit of the others. The leadership of the body of Christ, under the headship of Jesus Christ, is made up of many people each employing their gifts for God's glory. As each leader excels, he shares his leadership responsibilities with those who are gifted in other areas.

Psalm 23

1 The LORD is my shepherd;
   I shall not want.
2 He makes me lie down in green pastures.
   He leads me beside still waters.
3 He restores my soul.
   He leads me in paths of righteousness
   for his name's sake.
4 Even though I walk through the valley of the shadow of death,
   I will fear no evil,
   for you are with me;
   your rod and your staff,
   they comfort me.
5 You prepare a table before me in the presence of my enemies; you anoint my head with oil; my cup overflows.

1 Corinthians 4

1 This is how one should regard us, as servants of Christ and stewards of the mysteries of God.
2 Moreover, it is required of stewards that they be found faithful.

Isaiah 42

1 Behold my servant, whom I uphold,
   my chosen, in whom my soul delights;
2 I have put my Spirit upon him;
   he will bring forth justice to the nations.
   He will not cry aloud or lift up his voice,
   or make it heard in the street;
3 a bruised reed he will not break,
   and a faintly burning wick he will not quench;
   he will faithfully bring forth justice.

IMAGE OF THE SHEPHERD

From the life and death of the flock-keeping Abel, to the vision of the marriage supper of the Lamb who was slain, the Scriptures are steeped in images of the shepherd and the flock. There is little in the history and culture of Israel more familiar to them than the role of the shepherd.

Abram is called to set out with his whole household and all his belongings to go to an as yet unrevealed place of God's choosing. His travels take him through Egypt where his wealth increases even more, and he leaves there with many sheep, donkeys, cattle, and camels, and settles for a time among the Canaanites. The grazing needs of the abundant livestock cause strife between Abram and his nephew Lot, and the two men separate and spread out to avoid a family feud. The patriarch of the nation of Israel is a shepherd, and Israel is born as a nation of shepherds.

Isaac is rescued from the altar by God's provision of a ram. Jacob tends the flocks of his uncle and becomes a wealthy man in exile. Joseph is sold into slavery when he visits his older brothers as they tend the family flocks. Years later when the whole family joins Joseph in Egypt to survive the famine, he advises them to ask to settle in the land of Goshen because they are shepherds and the land of Goshen is rich and favourable. Four hundred years later, the multitudinous nation of Israel leaves the slavery of Egypt and takes their flocks with them. They are led by the shepherd Moses, who was raised in Pharaoh's courts but

18

matured over 40 years while tending his father-in-law's sheep on the other side of the desert.

At the end of Moses' life, after Moses has led Israel for many years, God reveals to him that he will not go into the promised land. Moses' concern for the well-being of the nation quickly surfaces, and he responds to God: "May the Lord, the God who gives breath to all living things, appoint someone over this community to go out and come in before them, one who will lead them out and bring them in, so the Lord's people will not be like sheep without a shepherd" (Numbers 27:15-17 NIV). The Lord instructs Moses to anoint Joshua, "a man in whom is the spirit of leadership" (v. 18).

The lack of godly leadership is likened in the Bible to a disastrous scenario: a scattered flock of sheep with no one to care for them.

Many years later, God calls a shepherd boy to lead the nation of Israel as king, and declares him to be a "man after my own heart" (Acts 13:22).

Chapter 2: Image of the Shepherd

The lessons David learned while caring for his father's sheep turn out to be his royal training. David leans on those lessons when faced with the ungodly challenge that the giant Goliath throws at the army of Israel, remembering how he protected the sheep from savage animals with God's help. Later, he pens the words of the best-known psalm: "The Lord is my shepherd, I shall not want…" (Psalm 23:1).

The lack of godly leadership is likened in the Bible to a disastrous scenario: a scattered flock of sheep with no one to care for them. The prophet Micaiah uses this phrase as he tells King Ahab of his impending death (2 Chronicles 18:16), as does Isaiah as he warns of the coming destruction of Babylon by the Medes (Isaiah 13:14). Indeed, a nation without godly leadership is as vulnerable as a flock of sheep without a shepherd. The leaders of Israel are repeatedly compared to shepherds, just as God himself is the shepherd of Israel.

Both Matthew and Mark record Jesus having compassion on the crowds "because they were harassed and helpless, like sheep without a shepherd" (Matthew 9:36; Mark 6:34).

Jesus the shepherd

In a profound discourse recorded in John 10, Jesus declares himself to be the good shepherd who will lay down his own life for the benefit of his sheep. Like God the Father, God the Son is the eternal shepherd of his chosen and called people. The relationship between shepherd and sheep illustrates the relationship God has with his people, and it sets the example that God has designed and commanded everyone who leads in his kingdom to follow.

When the risen Christ restores Peter out of his deep guilt and shame for having denied him three times, he confirms Peter's love for him and commands Peter to feed his sheep. This restoration of commitment, and the assignment from Jesus to be a shepherd of those who follow Christ must have been a driving force for the rest of Peter's life. Years later, when he writes what we know as his first letter, he calls God "the Shepherd and Overseer of your souls" (1 Peter 2:25) and "the chief Shepherd" (1 Peter 5:4). He passes on the shepherd assignment to the elders of the church: "Be shepherds of God's flock that is under your care, watching over them – not because you must, but

1 Kings 22
17 And he said, "I saw all Israel scattered on the mountains, as sheep that have no shepherd. And the Lord said, 'These have no master; let each return to his home in peace.'"

Ezekiel 34
11 "For thus says the Lord God: Behold, I, I myself will search for my sheep and will seek them out.
12 As a shepherd seeks out his flock when he is among his sheep that have been scattered, so will I seek out my sheep, and I will rescue them from all places where they have been scattered on a day of clouds and thick darkness.
13 And I will bring them out from the peoples and gather them from the countries, and will bring them into their own land. And I will feed them on the mountains of Israel, by the ravines, and in all the inhabited places of the country.
14 I will feed them with good pasture, and on the mountain heights of Israel shall be their grazing land. There they shall lie down in good grazing land, and on rich pasture they shall feed on the mountains of Israel.
15 I myself will be the shepherd of my sheep, and I myself will make them lie down, declares the Lord GOD.

because you are willing, as God wants you to be…" (1 Peter 5:2 NIV).

Since the Bible is so focused on the image of the shepherd as leader of God's people, we would do well to explore what that image would have communicated to the Jewish nation, and to the disciples at the time of Christ. Even more importantly, what does the shepherd image communicate to you and me who live in cultures very different to those of Old and New Testament Israel?

> *What does the shepherd image communicate to you and me who live in cultures very different to those of Old and New Testament Israel?*

Parables, metaphors, and similes are designed to communicate certain truths, and we have to be careful not to miss their meanings by being distracted with thoughts that are incongruent with their messages. The truth is that shepherds are by nature very different from their sheep. Shepherds are thinking, speaking, rational human beings, and the sheep under their care are dumb animals. However, it is a grave error for

any leader to despise the people that they lead, to consider them inferior beings who can be manipulated, or to believe they are in need of a superior caregiver. The leader in God's Kingdom is in no way inherently different to those he leads.

The shepherd also benefits from the produce of his flock. He shears their wool and eats their flesh! We would be wrong to think that the leader in God's kingdom is free to harvest benefit from the flock through their destruction, or to view leadership in the kingdom as a means of personal material enrichment.

In contrast, God confronts the shepherds (leaders) of Israel, through the prophet Ezekiel, for only taking care of themselves, for feeding off the flock rather than caring for it, for not strengthening the weak, healing the sick, or dressing the wounds of the injured ones, for not bringing back the strays or finding the lost, and for ruling harshly and brutally (Ezekiel 34). God promises that he will restore leadership by shepherding his people himself:
"'I myself will tend my sheep and have them lie down,' declares the Sovereign

Lord. 'I will search for the lost and bring back the strays. I will bind up the injured and strengthen the weak, but the sleek and the strong I will destroy.
I will shepherd the flock with justice'" (Ezekiel 34:15-16 NIV). God promises to send his servant David to shepherd his people (Ezekiel 34:23 NIV).

Jesus, the son of God, is the fulfillment of that good shepherd who came and laid down his life for his sheep.

Shepherd leaders

Like Peter, we are entrusted as leaders in God's kingdom to shepherd his flock and feed his sheep. Each of us who are called to lead in God's kingdom should constantly be asking ourselves: As a shepherd of God's flock, how can I lead in a way that pleases him?

The key concept of the shepherd image is care of the flock. The shepherd's purpose and goal is the well-being of his sheep. All of his activities are aimed at the growth, safety, and health of the sheep under his care. The focus is on the sheep and not on the shepherd. We bask in the security of Psalm 23 and the joy of having the Almighty as our personal shepherd. We have

experienced the love of the good shepherd as he has nurtured us, healed us, filled us with purpose and carried us in his arms. We have received the personal, sacrificial shepherding of our Lord. We merely imitate him as we attempt to be shepherd leaders to those he has placed within our care. The godly leader is entrusted with the care of those who belong to the chief shepherd, and the way we lead should reflect the care, personal sacrifice, and love God has for his people.

Unless the followers are secure in the love their leader has for them, the leader has not succeeded in aligning his approach with that of the shepherd.

Our role as leaders is to shepherd in such a way that those whom we serve are the focus of our care. If we allow our leadership to be focused on our own position, status, or success as a leader, we miss what it means to lead in God's Kingdom.

Therefore, the result of leadership should be seen in the growth, fruitfulness, and welfare of those we lead. Godly leaders focus on the purposes God has for his people, who have been entrusted to our leadership. The shepherd leader loves sacrificially. Rather than striving for mere productivity, those who lead as Jesus led pour out their leadership as an act of selfless love for their followers. Unless the followers are secure in the love their leader has for them, the leader has not succeeded in aligning his approach with that of the shepherd. The followers of a shepherd leader will know they are inherently valued for who they are, not merely for what they do. They will know they are cherished as individuals, that their best interests are safe, that they will be challenged to flourish to their full potential, and that even failure will be turned gently into healing, hope, and restoration.

As leaders in God's kingdom, we should ask ourselves how well we are doing in binding up the wounded, seeking the lost, strengthening the weak, feeding the flock, and protecting our people from harm. Are we acting in keeping with the example of our good shepherd, or have we slipped into patterns of behavior shown by the shepherds who were rebuked by Ezekiel?

Those we lead should be influenced by us to develop their abilities, grow deeper in their faith, and increasingly fulfil their purpose in life. They should feel safe under our leadership, knowing they are secure in their freedom to serve, grow, and flourish under our guidance and care.

If they were one day lost and in peril, would they be confident that their shepherd would search for them until they are found and safe?

There should be no doubt that that they are loved by their leader.

03 IMAGE OF THE SERVANT

Moses is repeatedly given the title of "servant of the Lord" in the books of Joshua and Deuteronomy. Joshua inherits the same designation (Joshua 24:29). King David is named as the servant of the Lord in the credits of Psalms 18 and 36. However, the central subject of the servant figure in the Scriptures is Christ, the Messiah.

Jesus the servant

The four servant songs in Isaiah foretell the coming of the Messiah as the servant of God.

Isaiah 42 portrays the servant as the one chosen, upheld, and delighted in by Yahweh. The servant's purpose is to bring justice to the nations (Isaiah 42:1-4).

In Isaiah 49, the servant is called before his birth to bring Israel back to God and to give salvation to the Gentiles (Isaiah 49:1-6).

In Isaiah 50, the servant is abused and disdained: "I offered my back to those who beat me, my cheeks to those who pulled out my beard; I did not hide my face from mocking and spitting" (Isaiah 50:6). The abuse Jesus suffered was part of his purpose as the servant of Yahweh.

Isaiah 42

1 *Behold my servant, whom I uphold,*
   my chosen, in whom my soul delights; I have put my Spirit upon him;
2 *he will bring forth justice to the nations.*
3 *He will not cry aloud or lift up his voice,*
   or make it heard in the street;
   a bruised reed he will not break,
   and a faintly burning wick he will not quench;
   he will faithfully bring forth justice.
4 *He will not grow faint or be discouraged*
   till he has established justice in the earth;
   and the coastlands wait for his law.

Matthew 20

25 *But Jesus called them to him and said, "You know that the rulers of the Gentiles lord it over them, and their great ones exercise authority over them.*
26 *It shall not be so among you. But whoever would be great among you must be your servant,*
27 *and whoever would be first among you must be your slave,*
28 *even as the Son of Man came not to be served but to serve, and to give his life as a ransom for many."*

The fourth servant song, in Isaiah 52:13 to 53:12, is a detailed prophecy of the sacrifice Jesus would make for the sins of many. The purpose of God's servant is salvation, through being the perfect atoning sacrifice for sinful man.

A triad of New Testament lessons on being a servant

The servant metaphor runs through the New Testament. Paul refers to himself as a servant of Christ and of the churches. He repeatedly refers to leaders of the church as servants, and he calls them to humility in servanthood. All of these references stem from the example and teaching of Christ. Three profound passages unpack the role of the servant of God, the Messiah, as he fulfills the prophecies and reveals the purpose for which he was sent.

1. The gospels of Matthew and Mark record in almost identical words the teaching Jesus gives his disciples regarding greatness and leadership in the kingdom of his Father (Matthew 20:25-28; Mark 10:42-45).

2. Shortly after giving this lesson, Jesus demonstrates it by washing the disciples' feet (John 13).

3. In Philippians 2, Paul explains in detail both Jesus' instructions and what Jesus did as God's servant.

Let's look at these passages in closer detail.

In Mark 8, Jesus begins to tell his disciples that he is going to be killed but will rise again on the third day. Soon after in Mark 9, Peter, James, and John witness the transfiguration, while the other disciples are left to continue the ministry Jesus had given them. They had been casting out demons and healing the sick in Jesus' name, but they were not able to drive out a mute and deaf spirit from a young boy. A dispute develops over this failure with the scribes just before Jesus and the other three return. Jesus drives out the demon, and as he and his disciples continue on their journey through Galilee, he again explains that he is going to die at the hands of the rulers in Jerusalem and will rise three days later. It seems the disciples don't comprehend the implications of this statement, and on the road to Capernaum they begin to argue over which of them is the most important. Jesus corrects them saying that the one who wants to be first must be last and must be the servant of all.

As they continue their journey towards Jerusalem, the mother of James and John asks Jesus privately to give her sons the choice positions of leadership in his coming kingdom. When the others hear about the request, they are indignant, not because they think the ambition of the brothers is out of place, but because they do not like the assumption that James and John are more worthy than they themselves are. Jesus, knowing he is heading to certain death, uses the opportunity to teach his

Greatness comes from humility rather than from pride, and from serving others instead of ruling over them.

disciples about greatness and leadership in the Kingdom of God. He contrasts the cultural norms of power and authority, wielded by the great leaders of the time, with the shocking declaration that in God's economy greatness comes from humility rather than from pride, and from serving others instead of ruling

over them. Leadership and recognition in God's kingdom comes from being a servant, rather than from recognized social position or the exercise of authority over inferiors. Jesus' words leave no doubt about his intentions: "You know that those who are considered rulers of the Gentiles lord it over them, and their great ones exercise authority over them. But it shall not be so among you. But whoever would be great among you must be your servant, and whoever would be first among you must be slave of all. For even the Son of Man came not to be served but to serve, and to give his life as a ransom for many" (Mark 10:42-45).

This instruction could not be more emphatic. "It shall not be so among you" is in the future imperative in many of the English translations, to indicate the importance of the command. In contrast to the worldly approach, in which leaders control the lives of their subjects, demand their obedience, and treat them as inferior, Jesus commands leaders in his kingdom to be servants not lords, slaves not masters. The difference between a lord and a servant, or a master and a slave, is profound. The former does as he decides, sees himself as more important than others, and expects others to do his bidding. The servant responds to the wishes of others, views himself as less important than others, and is attentive to the desires of those he serves. It is hardly surprising that the disciples do not grasp the meaning of Jesus' words the first time they hear them. Servanthood and slavery have little in common with their concept of a leader or a master.

Jesus washing the feet of his disciples with water is a glimpse of what he is about to do on the cross when he washes away sins with his own blood.

Not long afterwards, the disciples are with Jesus at the Passover meal, and Jesus demonstrates what he meant by the teaching he gave them on the road. He takes off his rabbinical clothing and dresses like a servant in order to wash the feet of his companions. Once he has dealt with Peter's indignation and over-zealous reactions, Jesus explains in greater detail what he has just done. Affirming that he is still Lord and Master, he explains that choosing to be a servant is an act of the deepest love one person can have for another. Again,

he commands them to be one another's servants and to imitate his behavior.

Jesus' act of washing the feet of his disciples with water is a glimpse of what he is about to do on the cross when, as the servant of Yahweh, he will wash away the sins of all mankind with his own blood. Although he is the almighty master, he becomes our servant and does for us what we are incapable of doing for ourselves.

Paul explains Jesus' humility and servanthood in Philippians 2. He writes, "So if there is any encouragement in Christ, any comfort from love, any participation in the Spirit, any affection and sympathy, complete my joy by being of the same mind, having the same love, being in full accord and of one mind. Do nothing from selfish ambition or conceit, but in humility count others more significant than yourselves. Let each of you look not only to his own interests, but also to the interests of others. Have this mind among yourselves, which is yours in Christ Jesus, who, though he was in the form of God, did not count equality with God a thing to be grasped, but emptied

John 13

3 Jesus, knowing that the Father had given all things into his hands, and that he had come from God and was going back to God,

4 rose from supper. He laid aside his outer garments, and taking a towel, tied it around his waist.

5 Then he poured water into a basin and began to wash the disciples' feet and to wipe them with the towel that was wrapped around him.

6 He came to Simon Peter, who said to him, "Lord, do you wash my feet?"

7 Jesus answered him, "What I am doing you do not understand now, but afterward you will understand."

8 Peter said to him, "You shall never wash my feet." Jesus answered him, "If I do not wash you, you have no share with me."

9 Simon Peter said to him, "Lord, not my feet only but also my hands and my head!"

10 Jesus said to him, "The one who has bathed does not need to wash, except for his feet, but is completely clean. And you are clean, but not every one of you."

11 For he knew who was to betray him; that was why he said, "Not all of you are clean."

John 13

12 When he had washed their feet and put on his outer garments and resumed his place, he said to them, "Do you understand what I have done to you?

13 You call me Teacher and Lord, and you are right, for so I am.

14 If I then, your Lord and Teacher, have washed your feet, you also ought to wash one another's feet.

15 For I have given you an example, that you also should do just as I have done to you.

16 Truly, truly, I say to you, a servant is not greater than his master, nor is a messenger greater than the one who sent him.

himself, by taking the form of a servant, being born in the likeness of men. And being found in human form, he humbled himself by becoming obedient to the point of death, even death on a cross" (Philippians 2:1–8).

Jesus, who never ceases to be God, chooses to make himself subordinate, emptying himself of his position and rights in order to be a mere human servant and to die as a condemned man.

We might protest against the demand that we emulate what only God can do, but we cannot miss the clear instruction

to avoid any trace of pride in our attitude towards others. As leaders in God's kingdom, we cannot hang on to attitudes of authority or superiority over those we lead. We have the injunction – and the freedom – to be servants and slaves of others through our positions of leadership.

In Philippians 2:9-11, Paul declares that because of Jesus' humility and obedience, the Father gives him the highest place of honour: "Therefore God has highly exalted him and bestowed on him the name that is above every name, so that at the name of Jesus every knee should bow, in heaven and on earth and under the earth, and every tongue confess that Jesus Christ is Lord, to the glory of God the Father."

If Jesus' leadership takes him right through the agony of the cross to final honour, is it not true that leaders in his kingdom will only receive honour through obedience and service, not through earthly positions?

Since Jesus is the fulfillment of the image of the leader as a servant, a leader in God's kingdom should look like the servant Jesus.

Servant leaders

Over time, the terminology of "serving as a leader" has become so commonplace that it has lost the impact Jesus' words had when his disciples first heard him say them. It is normal to speak of "serving as leaders", to call officials "public servants", and to

> *The servant identity is a lifetime identity for the leader, not a passing stage or a probationary period until that leader is promoted to a higher position.*

put on a servant tone in our speaking, without demonstrating anything that would resemble what Jesus meant in his teaching and by his sacrifice.

It is much easier to strike a pose of being the pious servant than it is to be dedicated to the well-being of those we lead. Our tendency is to begin to feel that, as leaders, we deserve prestige and authority because of the responsibilities we carry. When we are treated with less respect than we think we should have, we indignantly convince ourselves that we are worthy of greater honour because we are

the leaders and those we lead should honour us. All that remains of the image of a servant leader is the pious demeanour that is the stereotype of a Christian leader.

What does it really mean to live as a servant who has been given the responsibility of leadership?

It most definitely does not look like the worldly leaders who draw attention to their own importance, their power, or their "unquestionable" authority. Sadly, it does not look like the historical hierarchy that became the norm in Christendom over the ages or like some leaders in our Christian churches who want personal fame and recognition, to the point where it seems they themselves are more important to God's purposes than those they lead.

A godly leader does not look like someone who wants be a renowned leader, but much more like someone who sets out to be a humble servant. The motive of the first person is to become someone great. The motive of the second person is to live out his love for God and his love for others.

Isaiah 52

13 Behold, my servant shall act wisely;
he shall be high and lifted up,
and shall be exalted.

14 As many were astonished at you—
his appearance was so marred, beyond human semblance,
and his form beyond that of the children of mankind—

15 so shall he sprinkle many nations.
Kings shall shut their mouths because of him,
for that which has not been told them they see,
and that which they have not heard they understand.

Isaiah 53

1 Who has believed what he has heard from us?
And to whom has the arm of the Lord been revealed?

2 For he grew up before him like a young plant,
and like a root out of dry ground;
he had no form or majesty that we should look at him,
and no beauty that we should desire him.

3 He was despised and rejected by men,
a man of sorrows, and acquainted with grief;
and as one from whom men hide their faces
he was despised, and we esteemed him not.

Servant leaders are focused on the needs and the personal growth of those under their care. The servant identity is a lifetime identity for the leader, not a passing stage or a probationary period until that leader is promoted to a higher position. The godly kingdom leader

The core of being a servant who leads is a deep, unfeigned humility. It turns its back on selfish ambition and dedicates itself to the good of the followers.

continues to grow into greater humility and service, rather than into recognition and privilege.

In his 1970 essay, "The Servant as Leader", Robert Greenleaf published a practical guide on how to be a servant who leads. He listed 10 characteristics of the servant leader that unpacked his particular definition of servant leadership with a statement that has become iconic:

"The servant-leader is servant first.... It begins with the natural feeling that one wants to serve, to serve first. Then conscious choice brings one to aspire to lead. That person is sharply different from one who is leader first, perhaps because of the need to assuage an unusual power drive or to acquire material possessions.... The leader-first and the servant-first are two extreme types."[1]

For Greenleaf the test of servant leadership is how much those served grow and develop as people. He asks:

"Do they, while being served, become healthier, wiser, freer, more autonomous, more likely themselves to become servants? And, what is the effect on the least privileged in society? Will they benefit or at least not be further deprived?"[2]

His 10 characteristics are helpful, but they are not exhaustive, nor can they be seen as a divinely inspired checklist for a servant leader. But they do give us a good start in developing our leadership into something that looks like that of a servant.

As we consider our own leadership, we will do well to examine our motives, our pride, our responses to those who disdain and reject us, and our personal ambitions as leaders. If our own well-being receives more attention than that of those we lead, we can be sure we are not yet being servant leaders. If we are delighted in the growth and development of those under our care, if we use our influence and position to benefit our followers rather than benefit ourselves, and if we sacrifice our own rights so that our followers benefit, we could be on the right track.

The core of being a servant who leads is a deep, unfeigned humility. It grows from an inner self-perception which turns its back on selfish ambition and dedicates itself to the good of the followers.

We could ask ourselves who benefits from our leadership. If the health of our reputation and standing eclipses the well-being of those we serve, we may be reflecting the facade of the worldly leader rather than that of the servant of God.

"The first calling of every leader is to model out the servanthood of Christ."[3] "Everything else will come so much easier when we refuse the gravitational pull toward lordliness, acknowledging Christ as the exclusive Lord and take on the humble servant role as Jesus did from lowly birth to a crucifixion death."[4]

Isaiah 53

7   *He was oppressed, and he was afflicted,
    yet he opened not his mouth;
    like a lamb that is led to the slaughter,
    and like a sheep that before its shearers is silent,
    so he opened not his mouth.*

8   *By oppression and judgment he was taken away;
    and as for his generation, who considered
    that he was cut off out of the land of the living,
    stricken for the transgression of my people?*

9   *And they made his grave with the wicked
    and with a rich man in his death,
    although he had done no violence,
    and there was no deceit in his mouth.*

10 *Yet it was the will of the Lord to crush him;
    he has put him to grief;
    when his soul makes an offering for guilt,
    he shall see his offspring;
    he shall prolong his days;
    the will of the Lord shall prosper in his hand.*

11 *Out of the anguish of his soul he shall see and be satisfied;
    by his knowledge shall the righteous one, my servant,
    make many to be accounted righteous,
    and he shall bear their iniquities.*

IMAGE OF THE STEWARD

From the dawn of time, Adam, Eve, and their descendants are entrusted with the care of God's creation. Throughout the history of the nation of Israel and the church, people are the stewards of what belongs to God.

The concept of a steward was well understood in both Old and New Testament times, and it is very much part of our own cultures today. In the New Testament, the Greek word translated into English as steward, 'oikonomos' (οἰκονόμος), refers to the manager of a household. There were undoubtedly a variety of arrangements and contracts that placed someone in the position of household manager. He might have been an employee, a bondservant, or a slave, but his role as the person charged with managing the interests of the owner as a faithful administrator would have been well understood. The steward was not the owner but was accountable for managing affairs on behalf of the owner.

This image is found in several of Jesus' parables in which the steward is entrusted with the wealth, belongings, or business enterprise of the person he serves. The message in those parables is usually to teach the accountability we have in managing the affairs of our Lord. Both Paul and Peter give instructions to the believers to be good stewards of what God has entrusted to them.

Jesus the steward

Jesus makes it clear he has been entrusted with the will of the Father and, as a faithful steward, he fulfills his purpose. In John 6:38 he says: "For I have come down from heaven, not to do my own will, but to do the will of him who sent me." On the Mount of Olives, just prior to his arrest he prays: "Father, if you are willing, remove this cup from me. Nevertheless, not my will, but yours, be done" (Luke 22:42).

"Now it is required that those who have been given a trust must prove faithful"
(1 Corinthians 4:1-2 NIV).

The book of Hebrews quotes Psalm 40 as a prophecy of Christ coming to do the will of the Father.

Consequently, when Christ came into the world, he said,
"Sacrifices and offerings you have not desired, but a body have you prepared for me; in burnt offerings and sin offerings you have taken no pleasure.

Then I said, 'Behold, I have come to

do your will, O God,
as it is written of me in the scroll of
the book'" (Hebrews 10:5-7).

Jesus only does what the Father sends him to do. He is the perfect steward, faithfully and fully completing his assignment, declaring his work on earth finished, and then ascending to the right hand of the Father, where he intercedes for the saints. Once again, Jesus is the perfect example of what it means to be a leader who pleases the Father.

New Testament instruction on stewardship

In Matthew 25, Jesus tells his now well-known parable of a wealthy man who goes on a journey and leaves three servants to steward his wealth while he is away. On returning, the man reviews the servants' performance and rewards the two who managed his interests well, but severely reprimands the one who merely protected the wealth entrusted to him.

In 1 Corinthians, Paul corrects the believers for making their leaders out to be more than they should be by choosing to follow one leader over another.

The correct perception they should have of their leaders is as "servants of Christ and stewards of the mysteries of God. Moreover, it is required of stewards that they be found faithful" (1 Corinthians 4:2).

In 1 Corinthians 9:17, Paul writes: "For if I do this of my own will, I have a reward, but if not of my own will, I am still entrusted with a stewardship."

In his letter to Titus, Paul writes: "For an overseer, as God's steward, must be above reproach... " (Titus 1:7).

On that same theme, Paul writes to both Timothy and Titus about the qualities an overseer should have. One key quality is the ability to manage his own household, since "if someone does not know how to manage his own household, how will he care for God's church?" (1 Timothy 3:5).

Peter, meanwhile, instructs the believers: "As each has received a gift, use it to serve one another, as good stewards of God's varied grace: ..." (1 Peter 4:10).

Matthew 25

14 *For it will be like a man going on a journey, who called his servants and entrusted to them his property.*

15 *To one he gave five talents, to another two, to another one, to each according to his ability. Then he went away.*

16 *He who had received the five talents went at once and traded with them, and he made five talents more.*

17 *So also he who had the two talents made two talents more.*

18 *But he who had received the one talent went and dug in the ground and hid his master's money.*

19 *Now after a long time the master of those servants came and settled accounts with them.*

20 *And he who had received the five talents came forward, bringing five talents more, saying, 'Master, you delivered to me five talents; here, I have made five talents more.'*

21 *His master said to him, 'Well done, good and faithful servant. You have been faithful over a little; I will set you over much. Enter into the joy of your master.'*

22 *And he also who had the two talents came forward, saying, 'Master, you delivered to me two talents; here, I have made two talents more.'*

23 *His master said to him, 'Well done, good and faithful servant. You have been faithful over a little; I will set you over much. Enter into the joy of your master.'*

1 Corinthians 4

1   *This is how one should regard us, as servants of Christ and stewards of the mysteries of God.*

2   *Moreover, it is required of stewards that they be found faithful.*

3   *But with me it is a very small thing that I should be judged by you or by any human court. In fact, I do not even judge myself.*

4   *For I am not aware of anything against myself, but I am not thereby acquitted. It is the Lord who judges me.*

1 Corinthians 9

16   *For if I preach the gospel, that gives me no ground for boasting. For necessity is laid upon me. Woe to me if I do not preach the gospel!*

17   *For if I do this of my own will, I have a reward, but if not of my own will, I am still entrusted with a stewardship.*

1 Peter 4

8   *Above all, keep loving one another earnestly, since love covers a multitude of sins.*

9   *Show hospitality to one another without grumbling.*

10   *As each has received a gift, use it to serve one another, as good stewards of God's varied grace:*

11   *whoever speaks, as one who speaks oracles of God; whoever serves, as one who serves by the strength that God supplies—in order that in everything God may be glorified.*

▌ Steward leaders

The steward is possibly the easiest of the images to understand because we can identify with it so easily. We know what it is to work on behalf of an employer. We understand the importance of being faithful in the tasks and responsibilities we have as employees. In ministry, we know we are accountable to human authority, be it a board of trustees, a financial donor, or the person to whom we report. We understand that those we lead belong to the Lord.

Yet, sometimes as leaders we can become so invested in our ministries that our identity becomes entangled with the apparent success or failure of what we do. We can easily develop a personal "ownership" of the ministry, and of the people in that ministry, losing sight of the fact that we are merely stewards of something that belongs to God and not to us.

One way to help us keep a clear head might be to contemplate who will suffer loss if we fail. If our fear of failure is only for our own loss, then it might be that we view our ministry as belonging to us alone. When we understand that the success or failure of our leadership will impact the kingdom rather than just ourselves, we are more likely to manage our ministry on behalf of the Lord and not just for our own reputation.

In this sense, we have a new understanding of failure. We fail when we bring dishonour and shame on the name of the Lord, and we succeed when we accurately and faithfully reflect God in the way we live and lead.

Disputes between Christian leaders can create enormous damage to the testimony of God's kingdom. Such disputes are often driven by personal agendas, without real consideration for what the dispute will do to the faith of the people around them. For the sake of the kingdom, Paul exhorts us to "rather suffer wrong" than to bring dishonour on the name of the Lord through our disputes (1 Corinthians 6:7).

As stewards in God's kingdom, we should constantly ask ourselves whether we are faithfully responding to the challenges and opportunities of our leadership in a way that reflects our faithfulness in overseeing God's purposes, rather than serving our own agendas.

The central aspiration of a good steward is faithfulness.

Good stewardship requires skill. The leadership skills that help propel organisations forward in pursuit of their purpose fall into the category of good stewardship. Financial management is the obvious skill, but conflict resolution, vision casting, sound human resource management, legal accountability, good governance, team building, the rational and focused deployment of resources, effective delegation, guarding the reputation of the organization, remaining "mission true", good public relations, and so much more, are all part of the expertise the steward uses to faithfully take care of his master's home.

As stewards in God's kingdom, are we faithfully overseeing God's purposes, rather than our own agendas?

We dare not be inept or complacent in these tasks by trying to accomplish them without proper training and preparation.

Jesus the shepherd, servant, and steward

The shepherd loves selflessly. The servant personifies humility. The steward pursues faithfulness.

Jesus embodies these three images in all the fullness of their meaning in God's purposes and plan. He is all three simultaneously. All three images are different aspects of the same person. Similarly, his design for his people is that we are to be faithful shepherds of his flock, servants of those we lead, and stewards of what he has entrusted to us – all at the same time. God doesn't call some to be shepherd leaders, others to be servant leaders, and still others to be steward leaders. All kingdom leaders are stewards, shepherds, and servants. The focus of the shepherd is the well-being of those in his care. The desire of the servant leader is the development of those he serves. The steward seeks the best outcomes in the lives of those under his care and is accountable for the use and deployment of available resources. The three images are three views of the same picture, a portrait of what it is to be a leader who pleases the Lord.

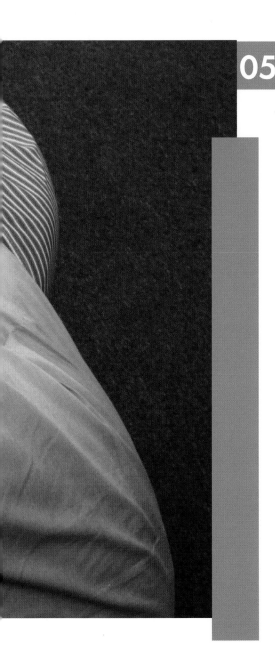

05 SHARING LEADERSHIP IN THE BODY OF CHRIST

How are these images reflected in the life of the leader in God's kingdom? As models of behaviour, the three images are startlingly different from the expected norm for secular leaders. The practical outworking is even more astonishing.

In Old Testament times, priests, prophets, and kings all bore the task of interceding between Yahweh and the people of Israel. In order to ask something of the Lord, an Israelite had to do so through those who were set apart to represent God to humanity, and humanity to God. These leaders were necessary intermediaries, as illustrated when, at Mount Sinai, the people asked Moses to intercede for them because of their great fear of God. God chose to work through specific people to speak to his chosen nation. Similarly, only at certain special moments did the Spirit of God fill individuals with his presence and power.

When the curtain of the most holy place was torn from top to bottom at the time of Christ's death, the barrier between God's chosen ones and God himself was removed. Jesus breathed on his disciples and said "Receive the Holy Spirit" (John 20:22), and then instructed them to await the coming of the Holy Spirit after his ascension. At Pentecost, the Holy Spirit was given to each believer, accompanied by spiritual abilities. Since that day, the

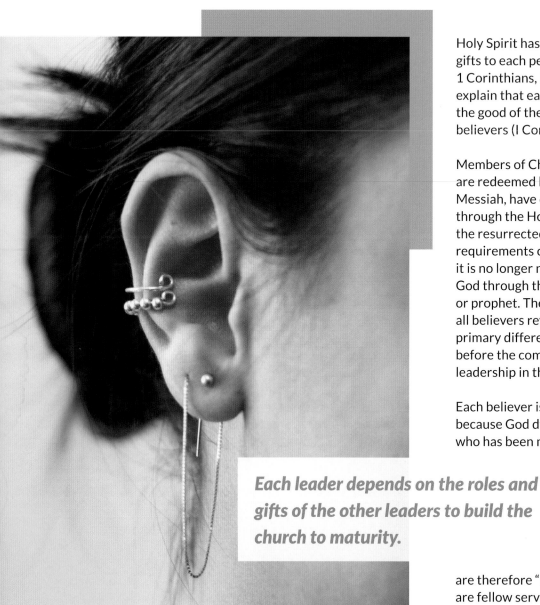

Holy Spirit has continued to impart gifts to each person who is in Christ. In 1 Corinthians, Paul takes great care to explain that each believer has gifts for the good of the whole community of believers (I Corinthians 12:4-31).

Members of Christ's kingdom, who are redeemed by the blood of the Messiah, have direct access to the Lord through the Holy Spirit and through the resurrected Christ. Unlike the requirements of the Old Testament, it is no longer necessary to approach God through the mediation of a priest or prophet. The "royal priesthood" of all believers revealed in 1 Peter 2, is a primary difference between leadership before the coming of the Messiah, and leadership in the church today.

Each believer is the temple of God, because God dwells in each person who has been made alive in Christ. He is our shepherd, head, master, and Lord on a personal as well as a communal level. Leaders in his kingdom are therefore "under shepherds". They are fellow servants and members of

Each leader depends on the roles and gifts of the other leaders to build the church to maturity.

Chapter 5: Sharing Leadership in the Body of Christ

the same priesthood as those they lead. Each one is entrusted with grace from above to serve the others in the kingdom. We are all given gifts as the Spirit determines, and each person's gifts are for the benefit of everyone, not just the recipient.

The image Paul uses to describe this remarkable reality in the church is the human body. The diverse parts of the body have different abilities and roles, each one specifically designed to be excellent at that role, each one placed to work in synergy and harmony with the rest, and each one essential to the vigour and vitality of the whole.

In Ephesians 4, Paul explains that church leaders are given diverse gifts and roles, all with the same purpose: building the church. The chapter starts with Paul's appeal to the church to live in unity based on the fact that we all share the same calling, the same faith, the same hope, and the same Lord. Paul then explains that those who are in leadership have different assignments based on the gifts God has given them. Some are apostles, while others are prophets, evangelists, pastors, and teachers. All are tasked with the same goal of building the church of God in

unity and into the full stature that God intends.

It's significant that the words "elders" and "overseers" in the context of the New Testament church are always used in the plural form. The only times

1 Peter 2

9 But you are a chosen race, a royal priesthood, a holy nation, a people for his own possession, that you may proclaim the excellencies of him who called you out of darkness into his marvelous light.

10 Once you were not a people, but now you are God's people; once you had not received mercy, but now you have received mercy.

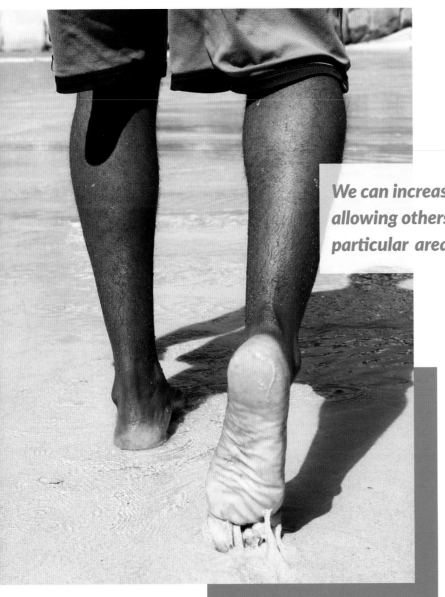

they occur in the singular are in Paul's letters to Timothy and Titus, in which he describes the necessary characteristics of an elder or a deacon. The New Testament churches do not seem to function with a single leader but with multiple leaders, each complementing the others through their different roles and gifts.

We can increase our impact exponentially by allowing others who are more gifted than us in particular areas to take the lead in those areas.

The leaders are committed to one cause, one purpose, and one goal under Christ. However, each has a different role. Just as in the image of the body with many parts, each leader depends on the roles and gifts of the other leaders to build the church to maturity. The evangelist depends on the teacher and the pastor. The prophet needs the apostle and the evangelist. No one is a complete leader graced with all the gifts required, just as no part of a human body is complete in itself. Shepherds, servants, and stewards in God's kingdom share their leadership in unity and common dedication to our one Lord.

Chapter 5: Sharing Leadership in the Body of Christ

The image of shared leadership is the image of the body of Christ under one head, flourishing as each excels in doing its part in humility and service of the others.

Sharing leadership

Sharing leadership is not easy. The difficulty lies not in the complexity of the concept, but in how challenging it is to apply. We are so conditioned to a hierarchical model of control and authority that we find it unsettling and threatening to allow another leader to take the lead with us. Since the leader is usually identified as the head of the body – and we all know that a body only has one head and that the head is in control of the rest – coming to grips with sharing leadership can be difficult. The problem lies in us forgetting that Christ is the head of the church, which is his body. Human leaders have no invitation to usurp his headship.

There is a powerful logic and a driving reason to share leadership in a gospel community. Since no leader has every gift required to lead perfectly, we benefit immensely when we allow and depend on others to share the leadership responsibilities with us as co-leaders and not as our agents. Imagine a leader who is exceptionally gifted in seeing the big picture, casting a compelling vision, and inspiring his followers to expect great things from God and to attempt great things for God. Imagine this leader also being adequately gifted in the administrative duties that accompany the position he holds, but not very good at caring for a hurting follower or nurturing the follower's spiritual resilience. It would not be surprising if this team made remarkable progress in achieving their purpose, but also suffered quite a high turnover of followers. Many might end up sacrificing their faith or collapsing under the wounds of life in the pursuit of the goal.

Imagine a pastorally gifted leader who struggles to take a decision to move forward because of his great concern for the peace and safety of his followers. How likely is he to lead his team to achievement and progress, rather than becoming inwardly focused?

What about a leader who can inspire action and nurture his team both in their spiritual vitality and their progress toward the goal, but cannot keep up with the necessary administrative tasks?

Ephesians 4

4   There is one body and one Spirit—just as you were called to the one hope that belongs to your call—

5   one Lord, one faith, one baptism,

6   one God and Father of all, who is over all and through all and in all.

7   But grace was given to each one of us according to the measure of Christ's gift.

...

11   And he gave the apostles, the prophets, the evangelists, the shepherds and teachers,

12   to equip the saints for the work of ministry, for building up the body of Christ,

13   until we all attain to the unity of the faith and of the knowledge of the Son of God, to mature manhood, to the measure of the stature of the fullness of Christ,

14   so that we may no longer be children, tossed to and fro by the waves and carried about by every wind of doctrine, by human cunning, by craftiness in deceitful schemes.

15   Rather, speaking the truth in love, we are to grow up in every way into him who is the head, into Christ,

16   from whom the whole body, joined and held together by every joint with which it is equipped, when each part is working properly, makes the body grow so that it builds itself up in love

Instead of simply managing our weaknesses, we can increase our impact exponentially by allowing others who are more gifted than us in particular areas to take the lead in those areas. Instead of recruiting helpers to avoid weaknesses in my own leadership, I can share the leadership load with others who lead in their gifting far better than I could, while I am at the same time free to excel in the areas in which I am gifted.

To borrow from the biblical image of the body, if the greatest gift the eye has is the sense of sight, it would do little good for it to try to improve in its ability to feel. Eyes do feel, but if they are touched, the usual result is pain rather than a comforting caress. Neither should the eye try to attend to weakness in its ability to hear, taste, or smell. It does not need to recruit the other senses so that its lack of hearing or smell won't be shown up as a weakness. I can stand on my hands upside down for a moment or two, but when I need to run, my legs and feet are designed for that purpose. We give freedom to the parts of our bodies to function as they are designed

Romans 12

3 For by the grace given to me I say to everyone among you not to think of himself more highly than he ought to think, but to think with sober judgment, each according to the measure of faith that God has assigned.

4 For as in one body we have many members, and the members do not all have the same function,

5 so we, though many, are one body in Christ, and individually members one of another.

6 Having gifts that differ according to the grace given to us, let us use them: if prophecy, in proportion to our faith;

7 if service, in our serving; the one who teaches, in his teaching;

8 the one who exhorts, in his exhortation; the one who contributes, in generosity; the one who leads, with zeal; the one who does acts of mercy, with cheerfulness.

He is likely to generate a happy chaos but shaky progress at best.

The obvious answer, which we all know and try to apply, is to gather people around us who are gifted in the areas we don't manage well, so that we can shore up our weaknesses and

Each leader is both the giver and the recipient of the blessing of the grace given to the body through the multiplicity of gifts.

mitigate the shortfall in our leadership. Good delegation is imperative, but in the leadership we are called to in the kingdom, it stops short of the image of shared leadership under our one head, Jesus Christ.

to function. Similarly, in leadership, we have the enormous privilege of giving freedom to leaders whom God crafted to excel in specific areas. In leadership, I can recruit an administrator to take care of my administrative needs, or I can release a gifted administrator to lead our followers, and me, in the areas of organizational order. I want the person who is gifted in nurturing the spiritual depth and passion of the team to nurture me too, even if I am the designated head of the ministry. As the designated head, I am able to allow others to lead me and do it far better than I would, without abdicating the responsibility entrusted to me. In fact, holding on to areas of leadership in which I am neither gifted nor skilled would show a lack of responsible stewardship of the gifts the Lord has given to the whole team.

Sharing the leadership means that the functions, the responsibilities, and the recognition of leadership are shared without jealousy or competition. It requires that some people on the team are more gifted than the designated head and that they share a deep and mutual trust. A wise leader will be attentive to nurturing the leadership gifts of those the Lord puts on his team,

so that both he and they can discover and release the benefit of those gifts.

Another aspect of sharing leadership in the context of a priesthood of all believers is that each leader is both the giver and the recipient of the blessing of the grace given to the body through the multiplicity of gifts. The leader in God's kingdom is not the one charged with dispensing God's grace to the others, but a fellow recipient of his

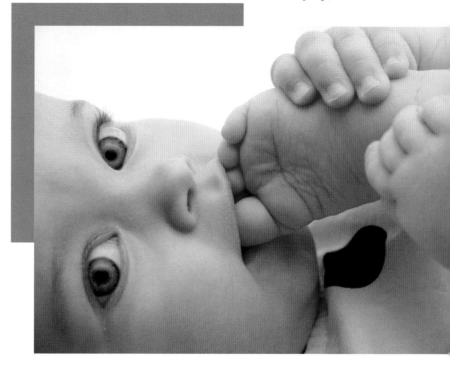

1 Corinthians 12

27 Now you are the body of Christ and individually members of it.

28 And God has appointed in the church first apostles, second prophets, third teachers, then miracles, then gifts of healing, helping, administrating, and various kinds of tongues.

29 Are all apostles? Are all prophets? Are all teachers? Do all work miracles? Do all possess gifts of healing?

30 Do all speak with tongues? Do all interpret?

31 But earnestly desire the higher gifts.

grace through the ministry of the body of leaders.

Organizationally, I don't think shared leadership implies an approach in which no one member of the leadership team can make a decision or move forward without the consent of all the leaders. A multi-headed leadership monster must be avoided. Nor do I think this approach allows the designated head of the team to abdicate any accountability or responsibility. The buck must still stop with the person who holds the position of team leader. A serious failure of stewardship will ensue if a leader does not remain aware and involved in all the leadership functions the position includes.

As the director of an international mission team working in the country of Paraguay (SIM Paraguay), I was blessed to have two very gifted men share leadership with me. Andy was a spectacular administrator. He was dedicated to the purpose of the team and to my success as the director. I asked him to lead me in that area, telling him not to ask my permission for any administrative decisions, but to definitely keep me informed of all that he did in leading and managing the affairs of the mission. I told him I would rather live with the few mistakes he might make than the many I would almost certainly make in handling government relations, banking requirements, property management, and more. I also promised never to undermine or question an administrative choice publicly, but that if I disagreed with something he did, I would talk it over with him privately, and we would come to the best decision in harmony.

Bob was a warm and caring man who had the love and energy to spend all the time needed to understand the concerns of the missionaries on the field. I asked him to nurture our hearts with his open and genuine love and care for each member, including me.

Sharing the leadership according to our gifts allowed me to focus on the vision, strategy and ministry approach of the team. I was also freed up to dedicate energy to the recruitment, orientation, and placement of new missionaries. By God's grace, the trust and esteem the three of us had in that season of leadership was never undermined or questioned, and that experience was one of my most formative as a leader.

LEADING the ETHNIC DIVERSITY of the KINGDOM

In the 21st century global village, most leaders find themselves leading ethnically diverse teams. This is increasingly true in the secular world. In a mission organization like SIM, leaders should not only expect to lead people from multiple nationalities and backgrounds but should become exceptionally skilled at it.

The triptych of biblical images of leadership that we have explored is both more difficult and most urgent to live out in contexts of diversity. Those powerful leaders in our cultures who lead by the force of their personalities, unbridled ambition, and arrogance are all the more caustic and ineffective in settings of great diversity. Additionally, gaps in our personal gifts and skill sets that may surface when we lead people from our own culture are all the greater when leading people from many cultures. Our blind spots become not just interpersonal but intercultural. The antidote is the genuine love of a shepherd, the authentic humility of a servant, and the conscientious accountability of a steward.

Acts 2

5 Now there were dwelling in Jerusalem Jews, devout men from every nation under heaven.

6 And at this sound the multitude came together, and they were bewildered, because each one was hearing them speak in his own language.

7 And they were amazed and astonished, saying, "Are not all these who are speaking Galileans?

8 And how is it that we hear, each of us in his own native language?"

In the midst of diversity, the biblical images of leadership are not only the most vital, they are also the most beautiful. The blended masterpiece of leadership in the images of shepherd, servant, and steward quietens the clash of cultures, while reconciling and redeeming the strengths and insights of each for the betterment of all.

A divinely designed splendour is revealed in the diversity we find in nature, in humanity, and in God's kingdom on earth. The creator clearly delighted in creating a universe that reverberates with variety in every aspect. Countless unique galaxies, spectacular geographical wonders between polar caps, flourishing ecosystems from deserts to rainforests, and breathtaking forms of living creatures fill God's creation, all declaring his glory. In God's design, humanity is also arrayed in the diversity of our tribes, peoples, languages, and nations. For someone in a position of influence, the easy route is to minimize or even squash this diversity with leadership models and formulae that standardize and homogenize. The harder and higher route for a leader is to magnify the diversity, choreographing the diverse gifts, skills, strengths, insights, and contributions into a symphony of productive work performed by flourishing people.

The biblical images of leadership have great relevance and application in the cultures and ethnicities of the world precisely because they are images and not models. Models impose a "one way is good for all" approach. Images evoke and instruct. Much of our understanding of leadership comes from our own experience wrapped in our preferred cultural blanket. Too often, explanations

Chapter 6: Leading the Ethnic Diversity of the Kingdom

of biblical leadership start with the context of the instructor, who finds an echo of his own cultural leadership norms in Scripture and builds leadership models out of it. Biblical characters behave in ways that are perceived by each culture in a different way. For instance, Nehemiah's leading of the returned exiles to rebuild the wall of Jerusalem is often seen by authors from egalitarian cultures as a display of great leadership skills shown by developing consensus and teamwork. Less egalitarian cultures may see evidence

A divinely designed splendour is revealed in the diversity we find in nature, in humanity, and in God's kingdom on earth.

of Nehemiah's powerful personality and his ability to show courage and determination as an autocratic leader sent with God's anointing and authority.

The beauty of the images of leadership is that each culture possesses similar images that faithfully communicate the love, humility, and accountability of the shepherd, the servant, and the steward. These images can be grasped and surveyed from the vantage point of all cultures without distorting their meanings. The messages latent in each image can be accurately discerned, contrasting with teachings on leadership which are often mired in cultural expectations.

Although only select cultures understand the role of the shepherd the in Middle Eastern patterns, all of our cultures have vocations that care, protect, nurture, and develop animals with the same purpose and love the shepherd has for the sheep. We all understand the role of servants, especially the humility associated with being the one who serves more important people. Each culture understands how one person can be entrusted with the material interests of another as a steward, and how that steward can be held accountable for the way he handles the owner's belongings. Dynamic equivalents for these images abound in our many cultures.

Similarly, Paul's narrative on the different functions of the members

Revelation 5

9 And they sang a new song, saying,
    "Worthy are you to take the scroll
    and to open its seals,
    for you were slain, and by your blood you ransomed people for God
    from every tribe and language and people and nation,

10 and you have made them a kingdom and priests to our God,
    and they shall reign on the earth."

11 Then I looked, and I heard around the throne and the living creatures and the elders the voice of many angels, numbering myriads of myriads and thousands of thousands,

12 saying with a loud voice,
    "Worthy is the Lamb who was slain,
    to receive power and wealth and wisdom and might
    and honor and glory and blessing!"

13 And I heard every creature in heaven and on earth and under the earth and in the sea, and all that is in them, saying,
    "To him who sits on the throne and to the Lamb
    be blessing and honor and glory and might forever and ever!"

14 And the four living creatures said, "Amen!" and the elders fell down and worshiped.

of the human body evokes instant recognition irrespective of our cultural background.

As we lead multicultural teams, we have the privilege of working out with them what the shepherd-servant-steward images of leadership look like in practice. The leader can explore clues to how people recognise that he is loving, humble, and accountable.

What in their cultural background would communicate to them that their leader loves them the way a shepherd loves and cares for his sheep?

The ultimate goal of biblical leadership is that God is glorified on earth, through the lives of his redeemed.

What in their culture would indicate humility like that of a servant?

What would be seen as faithfulness and accountability of an employee or steward? My suspicion is that these concepts play out in all our cultures.

The purpose of leadership

In much of the literature on leadership theory and practice, the definition of leadership is often expressed in terms of someone influencing a group of people in order to achieve a common purpose or goal. The focus is on achieving the task. The leadership function is to ensure that the goal is achieved by coordinating, inspiring, encouraging, managing, and making sure the followers perform appropriately. While it is true that all of these activities describe aspects of good leadership, a danger is that they reduce the followers to merely being the means to achieve a task. Although secular leadership has tended to place the task above the development of the follower, in more recent years it has rediscovered the value of the nurturing nature of leadership, rather than a single-minded focus on the goal to be achieved.

God's approach revealed in these rich images aims to transfer a leader's efforts of coordinating, inspiring, encouraging, and managing resources to an elevated level in line with God's over-arching purpose. A different dynamic occurs when godly leaders are modelled after shepherds caring for the flock, servants humbly attending to the needs of those they lead, faithful stewards responsibly managing God's kingdom, and leaders sharing their roles according to God's

empowering and grace. The pertinent question then becomes: What is God's purpose in biblical leadership?

It is significant that, as Jesus prepared his disciples to attend to the greatest enterprise in all of history, he commanded them to be his witnesses and to make disciples. He indicated that he himself would build his church. He would establish his kingdom through the obedience of his followers who are led by the Holy Spirit under one head: Jesus Christ.

The ultimate goal of biblical leadership is that God is glorified on earth, through the lives of his redeemed. The growth and development of his people is the key to bringing glory to him, as we grow into the purpose he has for us. The tasks and ministry goals we are called to could be just one of the means by which we develop and grow into what God has designed us to be. Rather than mere productivity and performance, God is interested in our spiritual growth and our true purpose, which ultimately is to glorify him.

May our determination to lead well truly result in God's glory and his approval of us as his good and faithful servants.

PHOTO CREDITS

Endnotes

1   Robert K. Greenleaf, *Servant Leadership* (New York, NY: Paulist Press, 1977), 13.
2   ibid.
3   Duane H. Elmer, *Cross-Cultural Servanthood* (Downers Grove, IL: Intervarsity Press, 2006), 161.
4   Duane H. Elmer, (personal communication, 2019).

Graphic design and layout by Simon Bremner and Carrington Haley

Cover design by Carrington Haley